God is Speaking
to Future Marriages

God is Speaking to Future Marriages

ASPIRATIONS

TRACEY A. JAMES

Copyright © 2021 by Tracey A. James.

Library of Congress Control Number:	2021916450
ISBN: Hardcover	978-1-6641-8976-8
Softcover	978-1-6641-8975-1
eBook	978-1-6641-8974-4

All rights reserved. No part of this book may be reproduced or transmitted in any form or by any means, electronic or mechanical, including photocopying, recording, or by any information storage and retrieval system, without permission in writing from the copyright owner.

Scripture taken from the King James Version of the Bible.

Any people depicted in stock imagery provided by Getty Images are models, and such images are being used for illustrative purposes only.
Certain stock imagery © Getty Images.

Print information available on the last page.

Rev. date: 11/19/2021

To order additional copies of this book, contact:
Xlibris
844-714-8691
www.Xlibris.com
Orders@Xlibris.com
831015

JESUS I just want to say Thank for being the Lover of My Soul, you are my Strength, and my Redeemer, thanks for guiding and keeping me you are AMAZING!

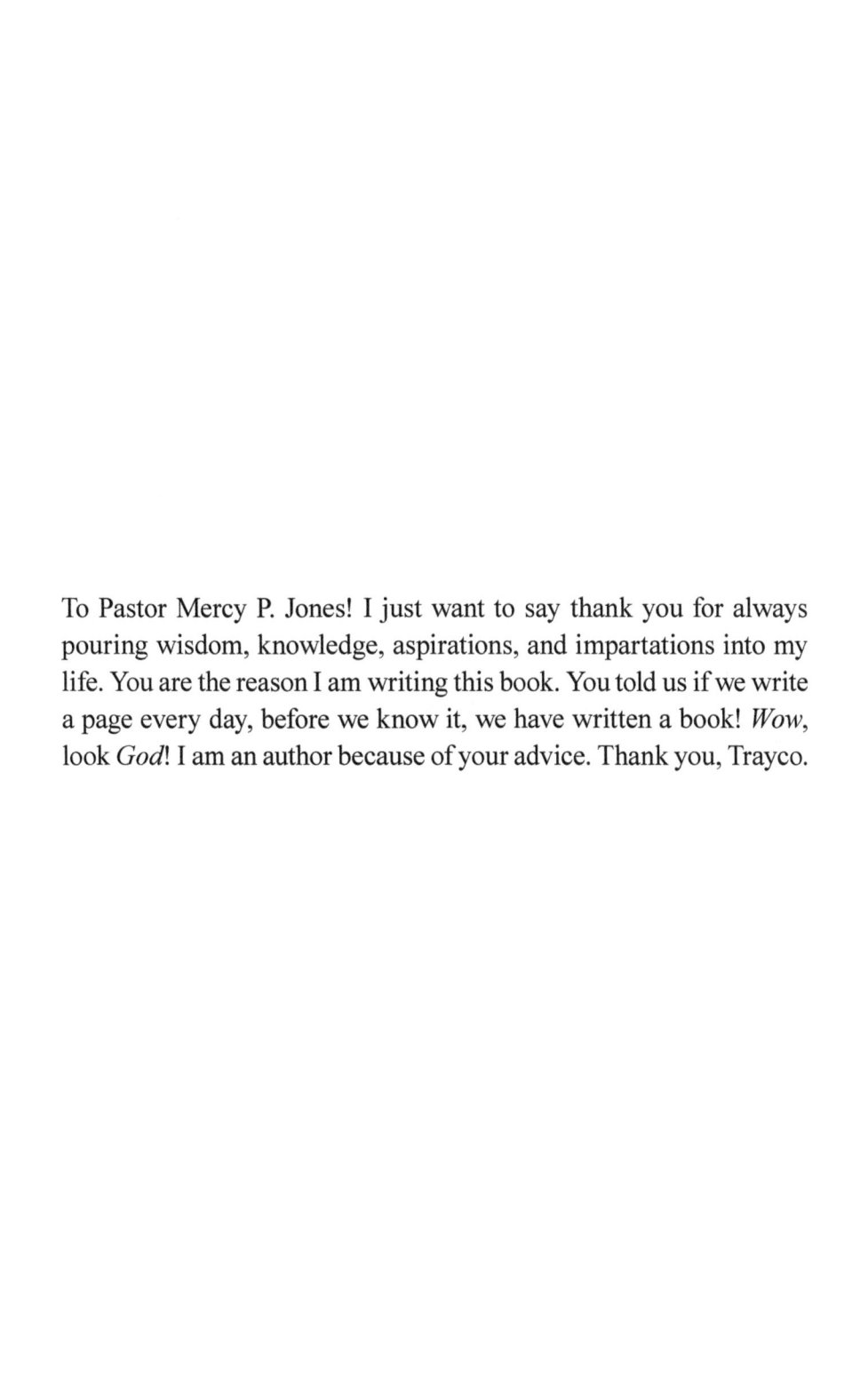

To Pastor Mercy P. Jones! I just want to say thank you for always pouring wisdom, knowledge, aspirations, and impartations into my life. You are the reason I am writing this book. You told us if we write a page every day, before we know it, we have written a book! *Wow*, look *God*! I am an author because of your advice. Thank you, Trayco.

Acknowledgments

To every single individual who contributed
words of wisdoms, thank you.

The victory is mine. The Lord is going to give me grace.

Hebrews 2:3

God is speaking to me loud and clear (Jeremiah 29:11).

Everything God is preparing for you is worth the wait.

God has heard your/my prayers and requests. The things you have been praying for are about to suddenly fall into place. He is going to amaze you with his goodness.

God isn't asking you to figure it out. He's asking you to trust that He already has. Jesus evening

Give me a song.

"All Is Well"

Troy Sneed

Humble yourself.

Trust God!

I will restore to you the years that the locust haten eaten. (Joel 2:25)

When we think it's too late, God whispers, "I still have a plan."

God is saying to you/me today, "If you saw what I was sending you, you wouldn't mind waiting. Get ready."

Let thy will be done!

Dear God,

Please bless my future spouse. Give him the strength to endure every trial that is leading him to my heart. Guard his heart until it's time to align us in your holy will. I just want to thank you in advance for him. And I can't wait to spend our lives glorifying you together. I praise you for the favor that will surround our marriage and for the beauty that will come from it.

In Jesus's mighty name, amen.

God is speaking to me concerning a future husband / marriages.

Sometimes you just need to relax and trust that things will work out. Let go and trust God.

Godly couples stay committed to Jesus and each other, period.

Imagine being married to a man who prays to God so he can love you correctly.

One day it will make sense why God took his time preparing your heart.

GOD IS SPEAKING TO FUTURE MARRIAGES

God will send you the one who not only pays attention to you but also pays attention to what God is telling him to do when it comes to you.

Be still.

Let go and let God.

If God wants you to be with someone, he'll make it happen at the right time and with the right person. Don't force it.

God has not forgotten about me.

God is speaking.

Don't worry, God is working it out for me.

Imagine a man so focused on God that the only reason he looked up to see you is because he heard God say, "That's her."

The man God has in store for you is just for you. You won't have to beg for his attention. You won't have to steal him from another woman. You won't have to *sleep with him* to keep him. You won't have to lie to him about your circumstances. All you need to do is be still and wait for God. Hallelujah!

Trust in God's timing. It's better to wait a while and have things fall into place than to rush and have things fall apart.

You deserve to be loved just as Christ loves the bride. You deserve to be pursued. Don't? For anything but the absolute best God has?

Title: God Is Speaking of Future Husband and Marriages

God is saying to you today, "You will suddenly meet the right person. Suddenly, your health will improve. Closed doors will open, new relationships will blossom, goals will be reached, and prayers will be answered."

Not my will, Lord, but yours be done.

Don't lose hope. Just when you think it's over, God sends a miracle.

Don't give up! Keep trusting in the Lord.

No matter what you have been through or what your current situation is, no matter what you have heard or seen, never stop believing that your heart's desire will one day happen.

Imagine a man on his knees praying that you become his wife. One day God will send you someone who chooses you every day for the rest of your life.

Strong men look to God for guidance.

You'll never be too much for someone who can't get enough of you.

Tell your man you are proud of him, you love him, and you need him. Sometimes appreciation is all that he needs.

And just when she decided to give up on men, she met a man who made her realize she never dated one before.

Everything is aligning for me. Trust it.

A man who is not after God's heart should not be after mine.

> For the vision is yet for an appointed time, but at the
> end it shall speak and not lie though it tarry, wait

for it, because it will surely come, it will not tarry. (Habakkuk 2:3)

God's timing might be sooner than you think. Be ready. Hallelujah! I'm ready, Jesus.

I just heard God say the best is yet to come.

You are a rare kind of person.

God created you to marry someone like you—*rare*.

Don't settle for less.

MOG, he's going to love everything about you.

Stand still and watch God turn that thing around to work in your *favor*!

> Whoever walks in INTEGRITY walls securely, but whoever takes crooked paths will be found out. (Proverbs 10:9)

Patience means trusting in God even when your circumstances haven't changed yet.

God is saying to you today, "I'm going to restore the years the enemy has stolen, the years you spent alone, the years you spent mistreated, the years you spent being neglected and abused. You are going to have plenty of favor, plenty of peace, joy, and miracles."

God is speaking of *aspirations*.

God knows what I need!

Relax. God wants you united with your spouse more than you do.

God, give my future husband strength to wait for me. Block any counterfeits that may distract him to lose sight of you. Lord, make sure his vision stays on *you* and he doesn't take his eyes off you, unless he is looking down when he finds me!

I'm the apple of God's eye.

> But let him ask in faith, with no doubting, for he who doubts is like a wave of the sea that is driven and tossed by the wind. (James 1:6)

A man of God (MOG) will know his wife by her spirit.

Sweetie, make me feel wanted and appreciated, and I promise, I will treat you like a king.

My MOG will hear compliments from me. Praise should always outnumber criticism in a marriage.

Just know that everything is going to work out. God loves me/you way too much for it not to!

> Look at the birds of the air: they neither sow nor reap nor gather into barns, and yet Your heavenly Father feeds them. 2:20 pm Are you not much more valuable than they? (Matthew 6:26)

Yes, I am.

God is removing toxic relationships and negativity from your life. *Love is coming your way. Money* is coming your way. You are going to be happier than you've ever been.

His undivided attention and affection even after he has married her.

She wants you to cover her, not throw them back in her face.

2 Corinthians 10:15

Mind of Christ

God is speaking.

The one God sends will make your soul blush and give you butterflies in your spirit. Pinch yourself. Could it be? Is this really happening?

My marriage will be like a fairytale per my sister Arsella.

> I will praise Thee, O Lord with my whole heart; I will show forth all thy marvelous works. (Psalm 9:1)

Wife, shower him with honor and respect, and a blossoming romance will be yours!

Be with someone who thanks God for your existence.

What God is about to do in your life will cause people to stand back and say, "Look what the Lord has done!"

12:53

Fairy-tale romances are just that! But Holy Spirit–derived premonitions are real and heaven-sent truth!

> But they that wait upon the Lord shall renew their strength; they shall mount up with wings as eagles; they shall run, and not be weary; and they shall walk, and not faith. (Isaiah 40:31)

Not only is God renewing your strength but he is also renewing your passion. What you've lost is being restored!

"I think part of trusting God is looking to the future with excitement, not worry and dread. We know that he is going to work out everything for His good, and in that, joy is found."

What you have been praying for is going to happen sooner than you think.

If you are reading this, you are not reading this by accident. You are going to make it. No matter what it looks like right now, God is going to send healing, solutions, blessings, love, and positive change into your life. So hold on, be strong, and don't give up.

Dance with God until he lets your husband step in one day. ☺ Sweet Jesus.

Never underestimate what God is doing behind the scenes.

Be still. The tables are turning, and it's about to get real.

God asking you to wait is another way of him saying, "Let me make the thing I have for you perfect!"

In seasons of waiting, you will be faced with exhaustion, and you will want to give up or, at the very least, lower your goals and *expectations*. But I want to encourage you to keep trusting God and keep expecting him to do the seemingly impossible on your behalf.

> But those who hope in the Lord will renew their strength. They will soar on wings like eagles; they will run and not grow weary they will run and not grow weary, they will walk and not faint. (Isaiah 40:31)

God is moving in the heavens. Take your hands off and let God be God in your life. He will take care of you and your problems. The promise may have been delayed, *but* you have not been denied.

My sister/friend told me last month that when we were helping set up Pastor Mercy's thirty-second anniversary, the pastor said this could be somebody's wedding. Vann Hodges looked at the front of the house and saw me and my MOG that today, *sixteenth of November.* I saw a bride and groom, and he had on a burgundy-colored hat. This is confirmation. I never send a groom on his wedding day (wow).

Lord, help me to be patient when I am waiting for your will for my life. Help me not to ??? ahead of the light you have shone before me. *Let me trust your timing completely.* Amen.

God is going to give you more than you asked for (Ephesians 3:20). God's plans for you are bigger than your plans for yourself. Don't settle. He has so much more for you!

We went on a fast, a consecration, on October 5, 2020. The Lord told me that he is going to show me signs and wonders to let me know that him who is speaking got another confirmation today that he told me last year.

November 16, 2020

God is saying to you today, "I am giving you signs everyday: in your sleep, on your timeline, in your conversations, in your music, on the television, on the radio, at work, in the sky. Pay attention to them and piece them together. You will notice a pattern." I'm communicating with you, my God, regarding my future husband and marriages.

November 17, 2020

God is saying to you today, "You're so close to your breakthrough. That's why the enemy is throwing everything he can at you. As long as you don't give up, you will reap a harvest. Your blessing is on the way!"

Hallelujah.

Look around. You'll notice signs that God is setting you up to bless you/me like never before!

Stop trying to rush things that you want to ask forever. God has a plan for you. Please be patient. Your blessings are coming.

Hallelujah.

Be patient.

You're about to overcome something you've been dealing with. Your mind and heart will soon be at *peace again*; everything will be okay. All things happen in his perfect timing. Say amen.

Someone is coming into your life, who is the answer to your prayers!

God is saying to you today, "You will suddenly meet the right person. Suddenly, your health will improve. Closed doors will open, new relationships will blossom, goals will be reached, and prayers will be answered."

November 18, 2020

Dear God, please help me/us, Lord, as we face the many challenges that come to our life. May you always guide us/me wherever we may be, and may you protect us from the devil's temptation.

> Marriage should be honored by all, and the marriage bed kept pure; for God will judge the adulterer, and all the sexually immoral. (Hebrews 13:4)

And when God opens this next door, you're going to understand why the enemy fought you so hard.

God has perfect timing—never early, never late. It takes a little patience and a whole lot of faith, but it's worth the wait.

> Trust in the Lord with all your heart and lean not on your own understanding in all your ways submit to him and he will make your path straight. (Proverbs 3:5)

God is preparing me/you for what you've been praying for!

Hold on to Jesus and trust the journey. He will never fail.

Be thankful to God.

Believe in what you pray for.

November 19, 2020

If God is making you wait, be prepared to receive more than what you asked for.

> Wherever you go and whatever you do, you will be blessed (Deuteronomy 28:6)

Get ready to hear "Congratulations!" God is not done blessing you!

Your season of rejoicing draws near. Be ready. Shalom.

God has a blessing with your name on it. Keep calm. Know that great things are in store. *God hasn't forgotten you.* You are blessed more than you know. Have patience and keep the *faith*. The biggest blessings come at the most unexpected times. Through God, all things are possible.

Your heart is precious to God so guard it and wait for the man who will treasure it.

10:00 a.m.

I declare *a fold recompense* because you have been caught, Satan, in the name of Jesus.

I still trust God.

>Take the helmet of salvation. (Ephesians 6:7)
The joy of the Lord is my strength.

I am so full; I am ready to pour out.

You may not understand today or tomorrow, but eventually, God will reveal why you went through everything you did.

>Be still and know that I am God!(Psalm 46:10)

God is speaking of *aspirations*.

Today, remember to be still and let God take care of those things that concern you. You have no reason to be anxious or worried about anything. You just make pleasing him your first priority and watch him bless you like never before!

Be blessed and be encouraged!

God has an amazing plan for me! Trust his timing!

Do you know you have already met a guy who saw a wife in you?

>Peace I leave with you; my peace I give you. I do not give to you as the world gives. Do not let your heart be trouble and do not be afraid. (John 14:27)

Yes, get hopeful and excited about the year 2021, but don't fall for the trap of thinking nothing great can happen.

There has been a massive shift in the spirit, and many will *experience radical testimonies* even in the remaining weeks of this year.

I pray that you will still have a mind-blowing testimony in this month of November. Amen!

> And all these blessings shall come on thee, and overtake thee, if thou shalt hearken unto the voice of the Lord thy God. (Deuteronomy 28:2)

If God wants you to be with someone, he'll make it happen at the right time and with the right person.

Don't forget it.

Divine meetings are being arranged.

You will be joined with a soul who wants what you want.

You may not always think alike, but you will always think together and love each other with the unconditional love of God.

> He said to me: "It is done. I am the Alpha and the Omega, the Beginning and the End. To the thirsty I will give water without cost from the spring of the water of life. (Revelation 21:6)

When it comes to the plan and purpose of God, *it is done*. It has been declared long before it has even started!

Remember that today, especially if you sense doubt is trying to creep up into your mind. Don't let the lies of the enemy cause you to believe anything that is not meant to strengthen your walk of faith. Know *that it is done*! Don't spend all day in your head, asking God how. Just be still and know that *it is already done*! Be blessed and be encourage. *Hallelujah.*

For we live by faith, not by sight. (2 Corinthians 5:7)
Prayer: Jesus, help me today to trust you more. Enable me to live by faith and not by sight. Amen.

It is not your job to catch a man. It's your job to serve God until he leads a man to you.

Be encouraged! God is working it all out for your good.

November 20, 2020

The goal of marriage is not to think alike but to think together.

God has already arranged your comeback from every setback, your vindication from every wrong, your new beginning from every disappointment.

Stephan speaks.

The attack has intensified because you are so close to the breakthrough. Don't slow down now.

This is not the time to stop praying. Keep praying.

November 21, 2020

The devil wants you to worry about what is next so you cannot enjoy what is now. He is a liar. Stop worrying. Always focus on God and enjoy every single day he has given!

You are about to meet "the reason" why God would not let you settle.

7:05 p.m.

You'll wait. You'll pray. You'll get frustrated. You'll question everything. But you'll continue to be patient. You'll keep waiting. And you'll keep praying. And one day, when you least expect it, it'll finally happen. So don't ever stop believing. Don't ever stop trusting. And don't ever stop hoping. God is so ready to give you everything you've ever dreamed of, but you have to understand it's on his timing, not yours.

Just because you don't see anything happening doesn't mean God is not working.

God is speaking of *aspirations.*

Your status is changing from single to married, in Jesus's name, amen.

Everything happens for a reason.

You may not see it now, but sooner or later, God will reveal why he let things happen. Always remember that his way is better than our ways; his will is beyond our will. Put your trust in him.

November 22, 2020

Keep calm and know the devil is a liar (John 8:44).

Someone is coming into your life who is the answer to your prayers.

November 23, 2020

Faith is trusting God even when you don't understand his plan.

I think Jesus uses our loneliness to show us that we will not find that everlasting, fulfilling love and joy from anyone or anything but him.

Amen.

And God said, "I am preparing you for greater. Get ready to go higher and deeper in me [God]. All your experiences, both good and bad, I will use for my glory. Claim it and receive it by faith."

Beautiful is the woman who sleeps alone at night; she knows her body is worth the wait.

Everything will happen for you all of a sudden, and you will be thankful you did not give up. Blessings are coming. Believe that.

Wedding bells are *heading your way.* Your *godly partner* is here. Hallelujah!

God is about to shift you.

God says everything in your life is about to take a positive turn. Do not give up. So many blessing are coming!

God is speaking of *aspirations.*

Your harvest is coming!

You're going to be surprised real soon at how everything suddenly and miraculously worked in your favor. You will realize how your current situation was only leading you to a blessing. Nothing is a mistake.

One day the *wait,* the lonely nights, and the *tears* you cried will all be worth it when you meet the *one.* God had him on *reserve* for you all along.

What God spoke to you is developing. You may not see anything improving, but if you'll stay in faith, what God said is on the way.

Someday you will be grateful that God gave you what you needed instead of what you thought you wanted.

Your prayers and petitions of love are being heard! Remain safe and full of godly joy, in Jesus's name!

You are not waiting to be disappointed. You're waiting to be blessed. Don't doubt God's timing.

#Worththewait

November 24, 2020

Stop doubting and believe. (John 20:27)
Today, don't let doubt take up *any* space in your mind. Without faith, it's impossible to please God, and we can't say we possess faith if we're walking around thinking doubtful thoughts. God is almighty and can do all things. Don't limit his works in your life by living in doubt. Be

Trust the direction that God leads you.

A husband can love his wife best when he loves God first.

God is speaking of *aspirations*.

Your next chapter will be amazing. God is changing your story line to one that's happy, blessed, and healed.

The very nature of faith is to give no room to doubt.

When God blesses you, it is different. Man-made blessings can't compare.

I do not know who needs to see this, but Isaiah 60:22 says, "When the time is right, I, the Lord, will make it happen."

One touch of God's favor can change everything. Stay faithful and trust in his timing.

> Thus Hezekiah rejoiced, and all the people, because of what God had prepared for the people, for it was done suddenly. (2 Chronicles 29:36)

God is about to change your story *suddenly*. You will go from *waiting* to *winning*.

Don't worry. The answers are coming. I am going to restore the years that you've lost. An unbelievable and unexplainable harvest is coming your way. I am settling the score. I am giving you back *everything* the enemy has stolen.

You won't have to beg a person to marry you, to stay with you, or to love you. God is sending someone who wants to marry you, who has love to give to you, who wants to grow with you, who wants all of you (flaws and all), and who desires what you desire in a relationship.

God has a blessing with your name on it. Keep calm. Know that great things are in store. God hasn't forgotten you. You are blessed more than you know. Have patience and keep the faith. The biggest blessings come at the most unexpected times. Through God, all things are possible.

November 25, 2020

Dance with God until he lets your husband step in one glorious day!

1:00 a.m.

If it is his will, he will make it happen. Don't give up!

God is speaking of *aspirations.*

Set the tone for *victory* by accepting nothing less than God's best.

Keep believing in God. Your days of dealing with counterfeits and time wasters are *done*. The next one will be *everything* you've prayed for and more.

Hallelujah!

> For He satisfies the longing soul, and fills the hungry soul with goodness. (Psalm 107:9)

When you meet a man who treats you like a queen, loves God, and looks at you as if you are the most beautiful woman in the world, he's your husband!

Love will find you, in Jesus's name!

Your secret tears will be turned to public victories. God is about to make you smile.

> Your word is a lamp for my feet, a light on my path. (Psalm 119:105)

Today, remember that when you do what's in the Word, God will do what's in the Word! In the Word, God promises that when we obey, we will have good success, be the head and not the tail, be most blessed forever, and will be safe in his arms. So no matter the situation, let the Word guide your actions and be a light unto your path.

Maybe you've been praying, believing, and being your best, but you don't see anything changing. You're tempted to live stressed but have a new perspective. You're in the waiting room. You're not missing out; you're not falling behind. You're right where God wants you. The promise is right on schedule. Now the key is to wait with a good attitude, not upset, complaining. "Father, thank you that what you started, you're going to finish. Thank you that what you promised is on the way."

> I know you have been lonely, but those days will end. In 2021, you'll finally meet the person I have chosen for you. Aside from myself, no one else will love you as much as that person will. You will finally find your happily ever after.
>
> Love,
> God

God is speaking of *aspirations.*

You deserve a love where you will never have to question their faithfulness because they are honest, loyal, and transparent. #Worththewait.

November 26, 2020

God knows when to send you exactly what you need! Don't give up hope. Prepare for what you are praying for.

It's coming!

November 28, 2020

> But as it is written, eyes hath not seen, nor ear heard, neither have entered into the heart of man, the things which God hath prepared for them that love him. (1 Corinthians 2:9)

God says before you overthink and overreact, pray! "Spend some time in my presence. I will help you."

You deserve a love where you'll never have to question their faithfulness because they're honest, loyal, and transparent.

> For he will order his angels to protect you wherever you go. (Psalm 91:11)

November 29, 2020

Never underestimate what God is doing behind the scenes.

There's still some who believe in that old-school kind of love, that "Let's get married" kind of love, that pure, honest, and faithful kind of love.

Stop looking back and checking on what you have already left in God's hands.

> Jesus replied, "You don't understand what I am doing now, but someday you will." (John 13:7)

God will restore to you the years that your last relationship consumed. The relationship ahead of you will be stronger and full of love. Soon, this season of darkness will end. Glory to God.

God is speaking of *aspirations*.

You are going to be surprised very soon at how everything suddenly and miraculously worked in your favor. You will realize how your current situation was only leading you to a blessing.

God is saying to you today that everything about your life is about to change for the better. Get ready. Something greater is coming!

Don't settle. Wait for the Lord.

I've heard your prayers. I've seen your tears. I haven't forgotten about you. Trust my timing. My timing is perfect.

God

You do not have to settle for the last choice! God will give you his first choice!

A safe man will come into your life and love you correctly. No sneaky stuff. No half love. No extra females. No inconsistency. Just you and you only.

You and your future spouse are meant to shake the planet together; you two have a beautiful purpose, and that is why the waiting season is so essential. Don't just wait . . . grow.

November 30, 2020

She deserves to be with a man who will not make her look stupid for being loyal.

The most beautiful thing a woman can clothe herself with is God's presence.

God does not want me to be a "fix him" wife. God wants me to be a "love him" wife.

The truest act of devotion to God is when you can lay down something in your life that you want to cling to so badly and trust that God will do what he said he would do. Waiting takes courage and patience. Waiting means putting your present desires aside for something greater down the road.

Be patient. God's blessings are perfectly timed.

God is speaking of *aspirations*.

If God is making you wait, then be prepared to receive more than what you asked for.

> Now all glory to God, who is able, through his mighty power at work within us, to accomplish infinitely more than we might ask or think. (Ephesians 3:20)

God is getting ready to send you a relationship that is beyond what you could ever pray for or think of.

You are closer than you think. Do not quit!

God has a purpose for your pain, a reason for your struggle, and a reward for your faithfulness. Trust him and do not give up.

December 1, 2020

God is releasing your miracle. You're going to receive everything he promised you!

The closer you get to your blessings, the harder the devil attacks you. Stay focused.

You will never be too much for someone who cannot get enough of you.

A blessing is something that brings you closer to the Lord. It is not things or money; it's intimacy with God. And blessings aren't meant to stop with you. They're meant to be poured through you onto others.

Are you waiting for God to fulfill a promise he made to you? Has so much time gone by that you are starting to wonder if it's even still worth it to wait? God sees you and knows how you feel, but just because you are feeling some type of way does not mean God is going to change his perfect plans for your life just to match your frustration or impatience. He told you he was going to bring it to pass, and that's what he's doing. What he's bringing together is better than what you asked him for or even thought about.

December 2, 2020

> Trust in the Lord with all your heart and lean not on your own understanding; in all your ways, submit to him, and he will make your paths straight. (Proverbs 3:5–6)

God is speaking of *aspirations*.

God does not want you to try harder; he wants you to trust him deeper. Stop trying. Start trusting. This will change everything in you.

God says, "This month, your sorrow will turn into joy, loneliness into love, and lack into plenty. That drought is coming to an end."

God will finish all he started. The delay will be turned into a miracle. Be ready to receive more than you asked for.

You're the woman for him. The possibility of losing you will never have to take place because when he has chosen you, he will want to treat you as his number 1 priority for all eternity.

December 3, 2020

God is not delaying; he is preparing you for everything you've been praying for. Trust his plan and be amazed.

> I will open the windows of heaven for you. I will pour out a blessing so great you won't have enough room to take it in! (Malachi 3:10)

God is saying to you today, "The pain, heartache, questions, and sleepless nights are coming to an end. I am going to open up the windows of heaven and pour out everything you've been waiting and praying for. Blessings of love, good health, and prosperity are coming your way."

Give me grace, Father, as I wait for my promises.

The wrong person makes you beg for attention, affection, love, and commitment. The right person gives you these things because they love you.

December 4, 2020

> Then the Lord God made a woman from the rib he had taken out of men, and he brought her to the man.
>
> The man said, "this is now bone of my bone and flesh of my flesh, she shall be called woman; for she was taken out of man. (Genesis 2:22–23)

God is speaking of *aspirations*.

> That is why a man leaves his father and mother and is united to his wife, and they become one flesh. (Genesis 2:24)

God is preparing you for something great. Just hold on and be patient. God's blessings are worth the wait.

Keep waiting for the one who makes you. Never wonder if better is out there, because in your eyes, you've already met the best.

This confirmation that God has heard over is coming. Get ready! Your prayer flow

Father, I thank you for my overflow. You are more than enough.

Good prayer (Jeremiah 29:11).

God is saying to you today, "You held on during the toughest of times. I gave you strength to endure that. At times, you did not even know it was me. When things changed for you may left you and wrote you off. But not only did you endure the storm, you grew in the storm. You are different. I did not create you to fit in. I created you to stand out. Now I am about to bless your faithfulness. I am about to take you to levels you never even thought were possible." In Jesus's name, amen.

To my future husband,

I'm praying for you, and I'm excited to pray with you for the rest of our days.

I do not want people to look at me and just see external beauty. I want them to say, "I see Jesus in her." I want to reflect his love in everything that I do.

December 5, 2020

> Rest in the Lord and wait patiently for Him; do not fret because of him who prospers in his way, because of the man who brings wicked schemes to pass. Have patience. (Psalm 37:7)

God isn't finished yet.

> Do not let your heart be troubled (John 14:1)
> Be anxious for nothing, but in everything by prayer and supplication, with thanksgiving, let your requests be made known to God; and the peace of God, which

surpasses all understanding, will guard your hearts and minds through Christ Jesus. (Philippians 4:6–7)

God is speaking of *aspirations.*

God is not only preparing *it* for you, he's preparing you for it!

Believe God is molding you for godly success and completion.

This was going to me last.

You can't see what God has been doing behind closed doors yet, but he is about to publicly reveal what has been privately in the works. God is putting your blessing on display so you can tell others what he is able to do!

It'll happen when you least expect it and in a way you can't understand. God is not man. Get ready for a blessing above and beyond!

Though single now, your next relationship is going to send shock waves in your circle and prove God is faithful to those who wait for him.

God is saying to you today, "You're about to be happier than you've ever been. Watch my next move."

And God said, "It's your season. I am about to blow your mind."

Desire a man who desires Christ.

No more mixed signals, no talking stages, no endless texts, and no games. Just godly, grown, intentional, healthy love. Your prayers have been heard in the heavenly realms.

December 7, 2020

Every time I thought I took a loss, God blessed me with something better.

The next one is coming into your life to stay. No more mixed signals or confusion; he will be sure about you.

Jesus is not the author of confusion or deception.

Your consistency will be your breakthrough.

We often get frustrated with our seasons of waiting for the Lord because we are waiting for God to provide us with what we think we need. The whole time, God is waiting for us to realize he is all that we need.

God is speaking of *aspirations*.

God is saying to you today, "Stay patient. My timing is perfect. I have something bigger planned for you, and trust me, you're going to love it."

Marry someone who wants to chase the Most High with you.

December 8, 2020

Never chase love, affection, or attention. If it isn't given freely by another person, it isn't worth having.

When you truly care for someone, their mistakes never change your feelings because it's the mind that gets angry, but the heart still cares.

Whose report are you going to believe?

Someday I will marry the right person for the right reason and with God's permission.

> The grass withers, the flowers fade, but the word of our God remains forever. (Isaiah 40:8)

That relationship hits differently when it is glorifying God.

Trust God's timing. It may not happen when you want it to, but it will happen.

Be patient and keep going.

> But Jesus looked at them and said, "With men it is impossible, but not with God; for with God, all things are possible." (Mark 10:27)

December 9, 2020

> I talked to your husband today. He's mighty handsome, he genuinely loves me, and he can't wait to meet your beautiful face.

> God.

What you do in your single season is what you'll reap in your marriage season. Plant wisely.

1. Trust in his timing.

2. Rely on his promises.

3. Wait for his answers.

4. Believe in his miracles.

5. Rejoice in his goodness.

6. Relax in his presence.

Everything God is preparing you for is worth the wait.

December 10, 2020

The wait is almost over. Those who wait for God shall not be put to shame.

> I will send down showers in season; there will be showers of blessing. (Ezekiel 34:26)

God is sending rain from heaven. Prepare for a downpour of blessings! You will receive everything you've been waiting and praying for. This is your time and season.

I'm worth it, always was and always will be.

Strong women are not simply born; they are made by the storms they walk through.

Choose a partner who is good for you. Not good for your parents. Not good for your image. Not good for your bank account. Choose someone who's going to make your life emotionally fulfilling.

I think part of trusting God is looking to the future with *excitement*!

> And he arose, and rebuked the wind, and said unto the sea, peace, be still. And the wind ceased, and there was a great calm. (Mark 4:39)

What a peaceful blessing it is to leave everything in God's hands.

Trust in God's timing.

It's better to wait awhile and have things fall into place than to rush and have things fall apart.

December 11, 2020

Keep praying. Your blessings are coming!

> A woman who fears the Lord is to be praised. (Proverbs 31:30)

> Watch, stand fast in the faith, be brave, be strong. (1 Corinthians 16:13)

God is speaking of *aspirations.*

Keep believing God for a man who's anointed to lead you, love you, pray for you, and be your best friend.

Your man is en route.

I want to marry a man whom I did not have to give a million chances to because he appreciated me the first time around.

You see what I carried you through. Wait till you see what I carry you to God.

Something you prayed for is about to arrive. The Lord has you in mind.

I hear keys. You will soon open the door to new opportunities.

> But they that wait upon the Lord shall renew their strength; they shall mount up with wings as eagle; they shall run and not be weary, and they shall walk, and not faint. (Isaiah 40:31)

Not only is God renewing your strength but he is also renewing your passion. What you've lost is being restored!

December 12, 2020

> Thus Hezekiah rejoiced, and all the people because of what God had prepared for the people, for it was done suddenly. (2 Chronicles 29:36)

God is opening doors for you that you thought were out of reach! There are great opportunities coming to you.

Suddenly, that will change your future! Your life is about to run over with supernatural blessings!

Something great and out of this world is being released to you! Keep going!

God is saying to you today, "Stay patient. My timing is perfect. I have something bigger planned for you, and trust Me, you're going to love it."

God wants to amaze you with the love he's bringing into your life.

God says, "You have been faithful. You could have given up a long time ago, but you didn't. I have seen you go without and still helped others as you suffered silently. I am going to reward your steadfastness and your faithfulness."

God is speaking of aspirations.

It's your time.

December 13, 2020

God got great plans for your future. Stay faithful.

Be okay with what and who God removes in your life! His replacement is much better for you.

A woman who found peace instead of revenge can never be bothered.

December 14, 2020

> Jesus said to her, "did I not say to you that if you would believe you would see the glory of God?" (John 11:40)

Girl, start acting like you are a king's daughter and there has always been a crown attached to your head.

> He who finds a wife finds a good thing and obtains favor from the Lord. (Proverbs 18:22)

December 15, 2020

> Do not be anxious about anything, but in everything by prayer and supplication with thanksgiving let your requested be made known to God. (Philippians 4:6)

> When the Time is Right, I the lord will make it happen You are going to reserve your mate quickly when the time is right. Change your relationship statics in this season. (Isaiah 60:22)

Be aware of the counterfeits by the enemy.

Pray for discernment.

Wait for God's blessing.

> And no wonder, for Satan himself masquerades as an angel of light. (2 Corinthians 11:14)

Seek the kingdom of God above all else, live righteously and He will give you everything you need. (Matthew 6:33)

God is speaking of *aspirations.*

December 16, 2020

Let God write your love story.

Love has a way of finding you and making you better. Lust has a way of dragging you and sucking the life out of you.

Love is coming your way.

Love isn't just what God does. It's who he is.

When God sends you the man he has chosen for you, you will know. This man will speak directly to your spirit and your heart. He will love you deeply and in a way that you have never experienced before

December 17, 2020

Woman of God,

The wife in you has been crafted by God to be a blessing to the one he's favored to discover you.

Ladies, it's not your job to catch a man; it's your job to serve God until he leads a man to you.

December 18, 2020

God has perfect timing—never early, never late. It takes a little patience and a whole lot of faith. But it's worth the wait.

Everyone deserves a person who can make his or her heart forget it was ever broken.

Do not chase what is not meant for you. Wait for what God wants you to have.

December 19, 2020

Dear Lord, I pray for your perfect peace to fill my heart. I pray you would remove any anxious thoughts and any fear that is in my heart and mind. Lord, please touch my heart. Overwhelm me with your peace. Comfort me. I pray for rest, and I pray that I can be still before you. Thank you for being my refuge. I love you! May your will be done, in Jesus's name, Amen!

God is speaking of *aspirations*.

Pray, then let it go. Don't try to manipulate or force the outcome. Just trust God to open the right doors at the right time.

Be honest of who you are, what you want, and how you expect to be treated. Standards only scare off people not meant for you.

Sis,

You are about to be so blessed. It is going to scare you.

Trust the process.

Stay patient and trust your journey.

Be with someone who says, "Babe, let's fix this. I can't lose you."

If it's for you, it will come to you. No chasing, no anxiety, and no stress.

What's for you can never pass you by. Trust the process.

Be patient, queen!

God is just preparing you. Be patient.

Singles, I am praying against the attack over your love life. The enemy will no longer hinder you from being found, being in love, or getting married.

While you are praying, God is preparing the love of your life. He will bring you together.

I believe there are five key things a man should consistently do when he has a woman:

1. Pray for her.

2. Protect her.

3. Love her.

4. Compliment her.

5. Actively pursue her even after he already has her.

I know it was tough, but God allowed it to happen for a reason.

December 20, 2020

Your soul mate will know exactly how to deal with you—flaws, mood swings, and all.

God is speaking of *aspirations*.

Pray that you and your spouse will be on the same page spiritually, emotionally, physically, and financially.

God is working things out for you.

December 21, 2020

He leads the way because he knows she'll always have his back. She backs him up because she trusts him to lead the way.

> The former things have taken place, and new things I declare. (Isaiah 42:9)

You have not been forsaken. God is preparing you for his best! Wait, I say, for the Lord.

I put all my trust in you. Lord, guide me as I seek to find your will for me today. Amen.

December 23, 2020

> May He grant your hearts desires and make all your plans succeed. (Psalm 20:4)

Live in such a way that those who know you but don't know God will come to know God because they know you.

> Glory to God in the highest, and on earth peace, goodwill toward men! (Luke 2:14)

Lord, teach us to speak gently, with wisdom, and always with love. Help us to sharpen each other and to help each other grow. Teach us to encourage with compassion and grace.

> Be still, and know that I am God; I will be exalted among the nations, I will be exalted in the Earth.

December 25, 2020

A great woman is going to challenge you. Not a single thing about her will be easy. She is gonna bring out the king in you.

God is speaking of *aspirations*.

December 26, 2020

Be patient.

Don't just throw yourself in a relationship with anyone because you don't like being single. Wait until the right one comes walking into your life.

When we think it's too late, God whispers, "I still have a plan."

There is a man patiently praying that he gets to be your husband.

December 28, 2020

Prayer has the biggest impact on your marriage. Use it as your everyday tool.

> Let us not grow weary of doing good, for in due season we will reap, if we do not give up. (Galatians 6:9)

You have been praying, and now he is coming to find you!

Be patient and let God make the introductions.

December 30, 2020

> Let us not grow weary of doing good, for in due season we will reap, if we do not give up. (Galatians 6:9)

There are too many of you living excessively, comfortably in relationships that are not honoring God. You claim to want and claim to pray for a godly relationship, yet you continue to be with someone who is not committed to marry you. Stop calling it a blessing while you're willfully living in sin. Do you really believe God sent you a boyfriend/girlfriend just to satisfy your flesh and loneliness? You created the relationship you're currently in.

Speak what you seek until you see what you have.

Love is patient; if that person loves you with the love of God, they will wait with you, *period*!

January 4, 2021

I pray you never again get attached to a man who isn't for you.

Sometimes you need to focus on growing yourself, and you run into what's destined for you.

God is speaking of *aspirations*.

Don't worry about finding him. Pray and God will make sure he finds you.

January 6, 2021

So many people get caught up in the details of their wedding day that they forget to focus on their future marriage. Planning for your wedding should be fun, but also invest in your future marriage by planning creative ways to love your future husband!

> God is my strength and power and he maketh my way perfect. (2 Samuel 22:33)

Pray. Wait. Trust.

January 7, 2021

I pray you get a man who loves you for the real you.

If you want a relationship that will last, make sure God is in it.

January 8, 2021

Wait for God.

Don't rush him. Trust him.

He is working everything out for your good and his glory.

January 11, 2021

> Marriage should be honored by all and the marriage bed kept pure, for God will judge the adulterer and all the sexually immoral. (Hebrews 13:4)

January 12, 2021

Strive to be a *Proverbs 31* woman in order to attract an *Ephesians 5* man so you can have a *1 Corinthians 13* kind of love.

Your desire to be married does not go unnoticed by your Heavenly Father.

The Word of God is the will of God.

You deserve a man who treats you right every day, not just when it's convenient for him.

January 13, 2021

May your husband locate you *this year*!

January 14, 2021

Ladies, place your heart in the hands of God, and he will place it in the hands of a man he believes deserves it.

January 15, 2021

Marry the one who understands that you and Jesus come as a package deal.

Let God work. Don't block your blessings by moving too fast.

When God is working on your behalf, be patient!

Good things take time! Do not get weary and do not get in the way!

January 19, 2021

The next one is coming into your life to stay. No more mixed signals or confusion; he will be sure about you.

I received that, in the mighty name of Jesus.

Marry a man who walks with God before he walks you down the aisle.

January 20, 2021

God did not create sex to be an audition for dating but a privilege only for marriage.

Marry someone who makes you fall in love with God every single day.

January 21, 2021

Lord, direct my future spouse to me. Destroy any distractions that may try to come against my kingdom marriage. What's for me is for me, and it will come to pass in your perfect timing.

You'll wait. You'll pray. You'll get frustrated. You'll question everything. But you'll continue to be patient. You'll keep waiting. And you'll keep praying. And one day, when you least expect it, it'll finally happen. So don't ever stop believing. Don't ever stop trusting. And don't ever stop hoping. God is so ready to give you everything you've ever dreamed of, but you have to understand it's on his timing, not yours.

January 22, 2021

God is speaking of *aspirations*.

Ladies, the way he loves and serves God will make a difference in how he loves you. Amen!

Wait for your Boaz.com.

January 28, 2021

Dear future husband, have a heart for God, and I would love you forever.

February 1, 2021

Dear future husband, I pray that we work as a team in furthering God's kingdom.

Dear future husband, God's about to do big things for us!

May you attract someone who speaks your language so you do not have to spend a lifetime translating your soul.

February 2, 2021

Genesis 2:22–24

The goal is to be happily married, not just married.

February 3, 2021

Matthew 19:4–6

If you rush it, you will ruin it. Pause, pray, and be patient.

A soul mate isn't someone who completes you. No, a soul mate is someone who inspires you to complete yourself. A soul mate is someone who loves you with so much conviction and so much heart that it is nearly impossible to doubt just how capable you are of becoming exactly who you have always wanted to be.

Wait for a man who will tell you, "I will never leave you, because I prayed and asked God to have you."

February 5, 2021

The goal of marriage is not to think alike but to think together.

Dear Lord,

Thank you for today. Thank you for our future marriages. Thank you for all the ways, big and small, that you are faithfully moving and working. We pray you would continue to grow us in our future marriage/relationship. Help us to be more humble, gentle, kind, and patient with one another. We pray we would take time to celebrate the growth we have already made and celebrate the victories in our lives. We pray our eyes would see the victories so that we do not overlook them. Victories made, prayers answered, hardships overcome, strongholds defeated, goals accomplished—they are all important, and we desire to celebrate and praise you for the wins. Lord, thank you for leading us and leading our future marriages, in Jesus's name, amen!

February 8, 2021

Dear future husband, I have been praying for you my whole life. I pray for you to stay pure and for you to stay strong in your faith. It can be hard, but I pray you take a stand for your faith and be unashamed. I pray for your parents as they raise you and the advice they give. I pray they teach you about God and how to be a gentleman.

Dear future husband, I haven't met you yet, but I already thank God for the man you are.

Until we meet,

Your future best friend

February 10, 2021

Keep being faithful to God. You're being prepared for a love story greater than you ever imagined.

"The beauty of the body of Christ is that each and every part is unique, your future marriages included, and God will use your uniqueness for his purposes if you let him."

February 11, 2021

A Prayer Partner

To every woman who is earnestly waiting for God for *her* MOG, the Lord will give you a "prayer partner." You will not marry a "prayer point." When looking for a spouse, please take your time to see how they will affect your spiritual life.

February 18, 2021

Dear Lord,

Thank you for your Holy Word, which guides us and gives us wisdom. We pray for more wisdom and more understanding of your Word. We also pray that you would give us more wisdom in our future marriage. We desire to be a wise couple as we make decisions together. We desire to honor you and honor each other as we walk wisely. Please help us in areas we are foolish and grow us. Please give us more wisdom that will benefit and bless you and our future marriage, in Jesus's name, amen.

February 19, 2021

Resisting Temptation

> There hath no temptation taken you, but such as is faithful, who with not suffer you to be tempted above that ye are able; but will with the temptation also make a way to escape, that ye be able to bear it. (1 Corinthians 10:13)

February 23, 2021

God is not only preparing you for it. He's preparing it for you.

Women who end up with an MOG glow differently.

Just wait and see why God had you waiting. What God is doing is beyond what you could ever pray or think of.

February 25, 2021

"A boy looks for a girlfriend, but a man looks for a wife."

I want the kind of love that has God's blessing on it.

A kingdom man does not settle for a girlfriend; he's in pursuit of a wife.

February 26, 2021

Fall in love with God first, and he will put the right person in your life.

March 1, 2021

There is someone out there praying to marry someone like you. You are someone's heart's desire. You are someone's answered prayer, and one day soon, you'll be spending the rest of your life thanking God for the beautiful marriage he has prepared for you. You'll see just how much God adores you when you receive the beautiful things he has spent so much time orchestrating just for you.

You are the woman someone is praying for.

March 3, 2021

God has a husband assigned to your future.

March 5, 2021

You deserve a partner who is not afraid to hurt other people's feelings to protect yours.

March 11, 2021

God will send someone who knows how to love and care for your heart.

March 18, 2021

Keep believing God for someone who will date you to marry you.

Always remember to *stay ready*; everything you've cried and prayed for is getting ready to *take place*.

March 23, 2021

A good mate will see your confidence as attractive and not intimidating. Amen!

March 25, 2021

When you believe God loves you, you can believe what God promises will happen.

March 29, 2021

Eventually, you will meet a person who is tired of the games too. And their loyalty

Inclusion!

I still trust and believe God. Keep the faith!

Index

Old Testament

Genesis
  2:22–23, *25*
  2:22–24, *43*
  2:24, *25*
Deuteronomy
  28:2, *13*
  28:6, *11*
2 Samuel
  22:33, *40*
2 Chronicles
  29:36, *18, 32*
Psalm
  9:1, *7*
  20:4, *38*
  37:7, *27*
  46:10, *12*
  91:11, *21*
  107:9, *19*
  119:105, *19*
Proverbs
  3:5, *11*
  3:5–6, *24*
  10:9, *5*
  18:22, *33*
  31, *41*
  31:30, *31*

Isaiah
  40:31, *7–8, 32*
  40:8, *29*
  42:9, *37*
  60:22, *18, 34*
Jeremiah
  29:11, *1, 26*
Ezekiel
  34:26, *30*
Joel
  2:25, *2*
Habakkuk
  2:3, *5*
Malachi
  3:10, *25*

New Testament

Matthew
  6:26, *6*
  6:33, *34*
  19:4–6, *43*
Mark
  4:39, *31*
  10:27, *29*
Luke
  2:14, *38*

John
  8:44, *15*
  11:40, *33*
  13:7, *21*
  14:1, *27*
  14:27, *12*
  20:27, *17*
1 Corinthians
  2:9, *21*
  10:13, *45*
  13, *41*
  16:13, *31*
2 Corinthians
  5:7, *14*
  10:15, *7*
  11:14, *34*

Galatians
  6:9, *39*
Ephesians
  3:20, *9*, *23*
  5, *41*
  6:7, *12*
Philippians
  4:6, *34*
  4:6–7, *27*
Hebrews
  2:3, *1*
  13:4, *10*, *40*
James
  1:6, *6*
Revelation
  21:6, *13*

Lightning Source UK Ltd.
Milton Keynes UK
UKHW012056040123
414846UK00012B/158/J